POCKET STUDY SKILLS

Series Editor: **Kate Williams**, *Oxford Brookes University, UK*
Illustrations by Sallie Godwin

For the time-pushed student, the *Pocket Study Skills* pack a lot of advice into a little book. Each guide focuses on a single crucial aspect of study giving you step-by-step guidance, handy tips and clear advice on how to approach the important areas which will continually be at the core of your studies.

Published

POCKET STUDY SKILLS

Janet Godwin

PLANNING YOUR ESSAY

THIRD EDITION

This edition published 2019 by
RED GLOBE PRESS

Previous editions published under the imprint PALGRAVE

Red Globe Press in the UK is an imprint of Macmillan Education Limited, registered in England, company number 01755588, of 4 Crinan Street, London, N1 9XW.

Red Globe Press® is a registered trademark in the United States, the United Kingdom, Europe and other countries.

ISBN 978–1–352–00610–0 paperback

This book is printed on paper suitable for recycling and made from fully managed and sustained forest sources. Logging, pulping and manufacturing processes are expected to conform to the environmental regulations of the country of origin.

A catalogue record for this book is available from the British Library.

A catalog record for this book is available from the Library of Congress.

Contents

Acknowledgements

I thank Kate Williams, colleague, series editor and friend, for her unflagging enthusiasm and support; colleagues who allowed access to materials used; the many students I have supported over the years for having taught me as much as I have taught them (and in particular those who kindly contributed to this book); my daughter Sallie for her common sense and perceptive illustrations; and my son Oli for his patience.

Introduction

It is one of the pleasures of working in a university study advice service to see students' marks improve as they begin to understand that there is a generic structure to writing essays. Students concentrate hard on finding facts and trying to 'write the right answer' when they are really being assessed on how they present their argument.

This guide is designed to be easy to follow and picks up the areas that most tutors say are issues for undergraduates at university. It aims to demystify the process of essay writing at university in a 'show not tell' fashion, and uses clear, concise text with illustrations, examples and tips included where this will clarify the point.

This 'quick reference guide' to essay writing covers the complete process: from planning the task, timeline and word count through analysing the question, structuring your essay, to the drafting and redrafting stages. Finally, there is advice about how to reference and use appendices, and then tips on how to use the feedback you get from your tutor. So try the book and see your marks rise!

How to use this guide

If you know what you are looking for, just dip in and out of this guide. For example, you may have lots of ideas but find it hard to structure your essay. For this, go to Chapter 7, which suggests structures for different types of essay.

However, if you find the whole process of essay writing at university a bit overwhelming or your feedback has highlighted areas needing development, then start at the beginning and work your way through. You can miss out bits you don't need for now, but as the guide is quite short why not just look through it all?

Janet Godwin

The purpose of essays

Essays are set so you can display your knowledge and understanding. They may have different formats depending on your subject. If you have been given a format to follow, make sure you follow it as closely as you can.

How does doing an essay display your knowledge and understanding?

Writing the assignment involves you in different activities that improve your understanding of the topic.

To write an effective essay you must:

- have a clear idea of what you are being asked to do
- gather information
- present your argument
- use the language and style most appropriate to the discipline you are studying
- do all this in a limited time and limited word count.

In doing this you will be using different academic skills:

- decision making to focus your work
- research skills
- planning skills to produce a logical argument
- writing skills used in a way suitable to your discipline
- time management and ability to work to deadlines.

What does your tutor want?

Your tutor wants to see that you have:

- addressed any *learning or knowledge outcomes* either for your course or this particular piece of work (p. 22)
- followed course or field *professional standards and conventions*, for example a business report format or addressing ethical issues for social work
- taken a viewpoint and *developed an argument* to support this
- *evaluated the evidence* you have found – ask if it is relevant, up to date and from a reliable source (p. 91)
- *shown a clear link between theory and practice*, usually by providing examples such as linking educational theory to actual classroom situations, maybe from your own practice
- followed academic criteria, usually *by researching and using a range of reliable sources* and *referencing these correctly*
- shown *transferable skills* such as *time management* and *presentation* of your work, for instance using a computer.

LOOK at your learning outcomes

The assessment criteria are designed to test the learning outcomes, but what does the term 'learning outcomes' mean?

The learning outcomes are what you are supposed to know as a result of doing your course. It is up to you to **show** that you have learnt these and **can demonstrate** this by some method of assessment. Helpfully, these are usually outlined for you in your course information or given with your assignment.

Example question: *How well does provision meet mental health need?*

Learning outcomes that need to be demonstrated for this essay:

1 Ability to create an appropriate psychological profile for the chosen service user that demonstrates an understanding of evidence-informed practice in relation to the issues being presented.
2 Knowledge and application of ONE social work theory and/or method to the process of assessment and intervention related to the service user.

Most students do not use the learning outcomes effectively. Learn to interpret these so you can target exactly what your tutor wants in a piece of work. It's a bit like reading your tutor's mind; your job is to match this as closely as you can. Learning outcomes are often written in difficult language so put them into your own words.

How students' and tutors' views of what is needed differ

It would be useful to know if students and tutors have different ideas about what is important in an essay. If you know what your tutors are looking for, you can match their expectations to maximise your marks.

Cover up the last two columns and put in order how important *you* think the different criteria are. Compare this with the results from Norton's (1990) research. If there are any surprises for you here, make a note of it now so you can check that your next essay matches with the tutors' views below.

Norton's (1990) students' vs. tutors' ranking of essay writing criteria

Criteria	Your ranking	Tutors' ranking	Students' ranking
Answer the question		1	1
Understanding		2	4
Argument		3	7
Relevant information		4	3
Structure/organisation		5	6
Evaluation/own view		=6	8
Presentation/style		=6	9
Wide reading		8	5
English/spelling		9	10
Content/knowledge		Not ranked	2

How do students' and tutors' criteria for a good essay vary?

According to Norton (1990), both students and tutors put *answering the question* as the most important criterion, but students thought content and knowledge was the next most important thing. Tutors, however, thought *understanding* and *argument* were much more important than, say, wide reading. This shows a key difference between the student and tutor perspective: your tutor is less interested in you displaying knowledge; they know that already. Your tutor **wants you to show your understanding by developing an argument using relevant information in a well-structured piece of work.** They are also interested in you having a view and being able to evaluate the quality of the evidence.

Take a look at the criteria Norton produced and compare this with your own view, taking care to notice any differences. These will be the *key aspects* you can focus on to improve your essay writing.

So this tells us you need to worry less about the content and more about **showing your understanding** and **arguing your own viewpoint.** Target these and you may need to do less reading overall.

Assessment criteria

You can see now that there are differences between students' and tutors' views of what needs to be in a good essay. This is important as the biggest difference when studying at university is that you **have to work out how to follow the assessment criteria for yourself**. However long ago it was for you, teachers at school did a lot of this for pupils, and assignments were designed so they exactly matched the assessment criteria. As long as the advice and instructions were followed, you were almost guaranteed to get it right. You may also have been allowed to submit a first draft, about which the teacher made helpful suggestions.

University is different. You may have just an essay question and assessment criteria, with no opportunity to show your work to your tutor before the deadline (which you will find is usually an absolute deadline).

For example: *Evaluate the proposition that a global monoculture will destroy diversity and difference*. Just where do you start? What exactly is your tutor looking for? How will it be assessed? This is where your assessment criteria are vital. They will provide clues to follow, and learning to interpret these will allow you to meet your tutors' expectations.

Have a look at your list of assessment criteria. The wording may vary but usually these follow the same pattern so it is worth looking at now.

Looking at *your* assessment criteria

Look at your **assessment criteria** now. Tick the ones in the table you are being asked for. This gets easier to do as you become used to academic language. It is important you get in the habit of checking which criteria you need to follow for *each essay* you start.

Tick the assessment criteria needed for your essay (then read the small print for each tick)	✔ or ✗
Addressing the question: does the essay clearly answer the question set and focus on the title throughout the essay?	
Essay structure: is this clear, logical and well defined with an introduction, middle and conclusion? Does the conclusion draw together points made in the middle and 'mirror' the introduction?	
Showing understanding: is this consistently demonstrated in a logical, coherent and lucid way with evidence of wider reading?	
Developing an argument: is this presented by a well-reasoned and supported argument based on the available evidence?	
Critical thinking/critical evaluation: is material presented in a critical manner, which critiques concepts or methods used and shows an appreciation of alternative perspectives and any current controversies? You may also have to critique the quality of the evidence you present.	
Use of language and academic style: does it provide a well-presented, readable and generally clear essay that the reader wants to read, and does it show correct spelling and grammar use?	

Adapted from Elander et al. (2006)

2 What you need to know before you do ANYTHING!

Preliminary groundwork

Before you do ANYTHING else find out the details listed below. A small amount of time spent finding these out now will save you lots of time later on when you are up against the deadline. This is your **preliminary groundwork**.

What?	Why?
Deadline date, time and place to hand in	So you can plan the stages of the essay to manage your time and workload effectively to *avoid an 'all-nighter' or last-minute panic.*
Word count or number of pages	This limits the amount of research done to what you can actually use. This *saves wasted effort.*
Format/structure	The tutor likes it done this way; they thought of it and if you follow this it *should address all the learning outcomes.* You would be mad to ignore this.
Percentage worth	*This limits the effort made to that required.*

Groundwork continued:

What?	Why?
Learning/knowledge outcomes	*So you can target these exactly.* Often these give you great starting points and suggest important areas you may have missed.
Professional outcomes	Many courses are designed to *train you up* in the *expectations of your future profession*.
Assessment criteria (just look at the ones **for an A** for now).	So that you *demonstrate research done* (theory) and *apply this* (usually by linking to practice or examples). Also to show you can *use and acknowledge a range of views* and show where you found these by *referencing correctly*.

The stages of essay writing

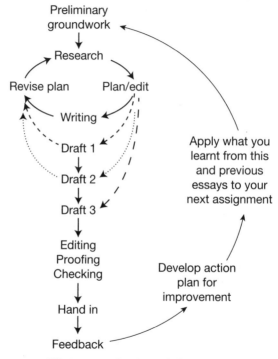

Preliminary groundwork

↓

Research

Revise plan   Plan/edit

Writing

Draft 1

Draft 2

Draft 3

Editing
Proofing
Checking

↓

Hand in

↓

Feedback

Apply what you learnt from this and previous essays to your next assignment

Develop action plan for improvement

What you need to know before you do ANYTHING!

Overview of the whole process

Preliminary groundwork *See page*
1 Find 'things you need to know' 9
2 Outline format (first plan)
3 Select and analyse question 22
4 Do outline task timeline 15

Research
5 Do an information audit 87
   a. What do I know?
   b. What do I need to find out?
6 Preliminary research
7 Further research (after planning/revising)

Planning
8 Outline format (see preparation above)
9 First plan (after preliminary research)
10 Adjust task timeline 15
11 Revise plan after first draft
12 Revise plan after second draft

Writing

Editing, proofing and checking

Hand in

Feedback

Next assignment? Consider:

- this essay
- other assignments.

Then apply this to future assignments.

Planning the whole process

You have a **set task** and a **limited amount of time** in which to complete it.

It is worth dividing up the time you have available to fit your time frame; adapt this to your particular strengths and build in time to cope with any difficulties you may have. The best way to do this is to do a **task timeline.**

You may be a good planner but find you always rush at the last minute because your work is over the word count. This happens because you do not limit the content of the essay to the word count available and so spend unnecessary time and effort taking out the research you so carefully collected. Or you may be dyslexic, so the reading and research will take longer than for other students.

A dyslexic student will have to target reading carefully and use strategies to decide when to read in depth or not, and then arrange for someone to proofread their work to check for errors.

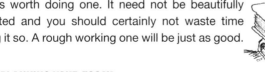

This means everyone's task timeline will be different, but it is worth doing one. It need not be beautifully presented and you should certainly not waste time making it so. A rough working one will be just as good.

Task timeline

Here is an example of a task timeline for an essay set on 1 November and due in on 27 November.

Time	Task	Completed
1-4 Nov	Preliminary groundwork Things you need to know Word/page count division Do task timeline Analyse question	3 Nov
2-7 Nov	Preliminary research	8 Nov
7 Nov	Plan	9 Nov
11 Nov	Revise plan/edit	-
7-10 Nov	Research	12 Nov
10-14 Nov	Write draft 1	15 Nov
14-16 Nov	Revise plan/edit	16 Nov
16-18 Nov	Further research	19 Nov
18-20 Nov	Write draft 2	16-21 Nov
20 Nov	Revise plan/edit	22 Nov
20-23 Nov	Further research and draft 3 if needed	-
23-26 Nov	Edit	24 Nov
26 Nov	Proofread	25 Nov
26 Nov	Checking	26 Nov
27 Nov	Hand in	27 Nov

What you need to know before you do ANYTHING!

3 Planning pays

What kind of planner are you?

Which of these describes you best?

Whichever one you are, you could do with a few tips.

I don't plan, ever

Ever heard of the saying, 'Failing to prepare is preparing to fail'? You would not go for a job interview without dressing smartly and trying to think of some intelligent-sounding answers and questions to ask. Without any planning your work will wander around and not really go anywhere. This will confuse both yourself and your reader. Planning helps you work through every step of the process with some purpose to ensure you use *all* the information you have been given to present an argument that actually answers the question.

All I seem to do is plan and not actually start the work

Overplanning can waste lots of time. You keep starting plans and then changing them. Producing nice-looking lists of what to do and coloured timetables or whatever makes you feel you are being a good student because you are working hard. The problem is you are *not producing anything your tutor can actually assess.* Every stage of your planning should be moving you closer to the finished product – your essay. This is why you need to consider first doing a task line (see p. 15), so that you keep moving on to the next stage.

I do plan but I never stick to it

This usually results in you not answering the original question – perhaps by answering the question you would like to have been set. Good analysis of the question and looking at the assessment criteria and learning outcomes will make you more confident in your plan. Your plan can, of course, be adapted as you go along. Any changes must be checked to make sure you can fulfil all the criteria, and then double-check you are still answering the question.

I keep changing my mind, so I can't plan

This often happens, and it results from lack of confidence about what you have to do. After dividing up your word or page count, *focus only on the information you have from analysing the question, learning outcomes and assessment criteria.* You may, of course, do a few outline plans as you work through your ideas, but you should soon be able to see which one would be more interesting to do. If you are still unable to decide, choose the one you can find the best evidence for, even if it is a less interesting one.

Becoming a better planner really will save you lots of time and effort.

Planning your planning!

To keep on target, your plan will have to develop throughout the essay-writing process:

▸ **Start** by dividing up your *word count* and follow any *structure or format* you have been given.
▸ **Next**, progress your plan by *analysing the question* (see p. 22), and refer to *your learning and any professional outcomes* and the *assessment criteria* (see p. 7).

- **Next,** you need to do an *information audit* (see p. 87) to work out what you already know and what you will need to research.
- **Now** you will be able to *start to structure your essay* (see pp. 30 and 59 and Chapter 7). Don't worry about this changing later on; this is a normal part of the planning process.
- **Lastly,** remember you will be *reviewing your plan* after your *first and second drafts*, so you do not have to have a final or perfect plan ready now.

Dividing up the word count

Don't worry. This is very simple and won't involve any serious thinking for now. We are simply going to look at some of the requirements needed for the essay and set out a very basic plan.

Requirements

Word count (or number of pages) allowed
Format or structure (if given)

Method

Take the word count and divide it up as follows:

10% for the **introduction**
80% for the **main body**
10% for the **conclusion**

So **for a 2,000 word essay** you will have:

> **200 words** for the **introduction** (knock off a nought to get 10%: 2,00Ø), and also
> **200 words** for the **conclusion**, leaving
> 2,000 − 400 = **1,600 words** for the **main body**.

Dividing up the page count

If you are using pages, do a similar calculation. Thus, for eight pages you would use a bit less than one page each for both the introduction and conclusion, leaving six to seven pages for the main body.

So now your plan will look a bit like this:

Introduction	10%	200 words
Main body	80%	1,600 words
Conclusion	10%	200 words

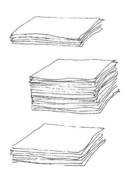

Dividing up the main body

The next step is to divide up the main body. If you have been given any **format or structure** to work to, you should look at it now. Headings or sections may already have been suggested. The best advice is to follow this format since it has been designed by your tutor to produce just what they want to see in the essay. Alternatively, look at Chapter 7 for different types of essays and suggested structures for these to see if there is one you can use or adapt.

Your **word count is your budget** and you can use any variation that adds up to this for your main body, but **don't overspend** as that will use up valuable time (and effort) later 'making it fit' the word count.

Using our 2,000 word example, we have **1,600 words** to spend, so this may be:

2 x 800	word sections	(divided into paragraphs)
4 x 400	word sections	
5 x 300ish	word sections	

The next step is to **analyse the question** (p. 22) and gather together any **learning and professional outcomes** (p. 10) and **assessment criteria**.

Analysing the question

In order to answer the question you first need to understand what you are being asked to do. There are **different types of words** in the title. A few easy steps making sense of these can help you work out all the clues in the question.

Helpful types of words in the question

Word type	Example	Function
Process words, sometimes called the instruction, direction or keyword	'Discuss', 'evaluate', 'critically analyse', 'briefly outline'.	Tells you the **process** you have to do; also indicates depth of research required.
Subject or **content** words	The main area under discussion.	Broad focus of answer (try to stick to only this).
Limiting or **scope** words	Dates, geographical area, number of examples.	Focuses the area to be examined; note this carefully.
Other **significant** words – key aspects	Any other aspects not covered above.	Identify the limit or scope of the answer.

Adapted from Williams (1995)

Breaking down the question

Use highlighters or box and underline, as shown below, to identify the different words in the question.

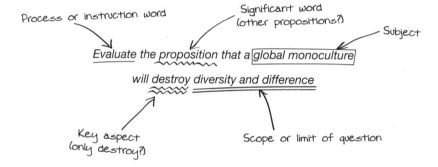

Process or instruction word

Significant word (other propositions?)

Subject

Evaluate the proposition that a global monoculture

will destroy diversity and difference

Key aspect (only destroy?)

Scope or limit of question

Assessment instruction (or process) words

These words tell you the **process** you have to follow and indicate the depth of research needed. You will not need all of them – just make sure you understand the ones you are usually asked for.

Word(s)	Meaning
Account for	Give reasons for.
Analyse	Break down into parts and examine, giving in-depth explanations. Show why these are important and how they relate or connect to each other.
Argue	Give the case FOR or AGAINST by using the evidence for different perspectives to support your case.
Assess	Identify strengths and weaknesses. Make sure you come to a judgement.
Comment	Show you understand the topic, give your view, do provide evidence and examples.
Compare	Show similarities and differences.
Contrast	Show how subjects are different.
Critically analyse	Identify the main issues from your reading, evaluate the quality of the evidence, come to your own conclusion and show your reader how you got there.

Word(s)	Meaning
Critically evaluate	Weigh up the arguments for and against; assess the strengths, weaknesses and evidence for both sides. Support with models, approaches and/or theories. Do make a decision!
Criticise	This is *not* about finding fault with a study or approach! Show that you can see the strengths and weaknesses of a view/theory and indicate where you stand. You must provide evidence, discuss this and draw a conclusion.
Define	Give clear, concise meanings. Show the limits of these.
Describe	Outline the main features. Keep it short; this is quite often only the first part of a question.
Discuss	Identify significant features, show reasons for and against and the implications of these.
Distinguish	Show differences between subjects.
Evaluate	Notice the word 'value' in 'evaluate'. Weigh up strengths and weaknesses and assess. Look at limitations, costs/benefits. Come to a judgement.
Examine	Look closely at, in detail.
Explain	Make clear and give details about how and why something is so. Give reasons.

Assessment instruction (or process) words continued:

Word(s)	Meaning
How far/to what extent	Set out the arguments and evidence on both sides. Your conclusion will be somewhere between 'all' and 'nothing'. Be clear about precisely where you are, and why/how you reached this conclusion.
Illustrate	Give clear examples and/or evidence to make your point clear.
Indicate	Point out, identify and clarify.
Interpret	Simplify; show what something might mean – especially data. Then make your own judgement.
Justify	Take a viewpoint and argue this, providing reasons and evidence.
Outline	Main features only; this is usually the first part of a two-part question, designed to check you understand a concept.
Prove	Establish that something is true with evidence and a clear argument.
Reflect	Examine an incident or experience. Look back at how you reacted, what went well or not so well, and what you would do differently in future.
Review	Examine critically, provide analysis and comment on important points.
State	Give brief, clear information. You do not usually need to give details or examples.
Summarise	Provide main points in brief, in your own words. The purpose is to show you understand the material.
Trace	Show the sequence of how something happened or developed.

Analysing the question for keywords to start your literature research

Very soon you will be wanting to start your research. Start by identifying **keywords** in your title:

Evaluate the proposition that <u>global monoculture</u> will destroy <u>diversity</u> and <u>difference</u>.

You need to both broaden and narrow the focus of your keywords. Have a quick think about this and then use synonyms, a dictionary or thesaurus such as www.dictionary.com to add to your list. Don't forget alternative spellings: monoculture, mono culture.

▶ For a **narrower** focus: just use *monoculture*; in databases you can limit your search by selecting articles written in particular years or a range of years.
▶ For a **broader** focus: include synonyms for diversity such as *change*, *difference*, *variation*, *similarity*, and alternative spellings or words for monoculture such as *mono culture*, *monocropping*, *mono cropping*.

Use **Boolean operators** and **truncation** to limit or widen your search.

Boolean operators AND, OR and NOT are useful to narrow or widen your search.

This example is from the Boolean Machine: http://kathyschrock.net/rbs3k/boolean.

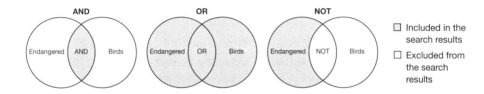

☐ Included in the search results

☐ Excluded from the search results

Truncation: Missing off the end of a word – truncation – widens the search area. For example, using the keyword 'employ' will find 'employee', 'employer' and 'employment'. Some databases use * to indicate this, so enter the keyword 'employ*' to get all the possible endings.

Sticking to the question

A common worry for students is whether they are answering the question. It is easy to get lost in all the detail of the essay and lose track of where you are.

Try using this technique to see if you have addressed the question and are working towards your conclusion.

At the end of each paragraph, look back at the question again:

1 Can you see how the paragraph relates to the question? Has it developed your reader's understanding?

2 Is it moving towards your conclusion? Note this down at the end of your essay in preparation for writing the conclusion.

If you can't see how the paragraph looks back to the question and feeds forward to the conclusion, consider if the paragraph needs to be there at all. (See 'Problem solving', p. 121 .)

Analysing the structure

Think of your essay as parts of a puzzle that are linked but have independent roles to play.

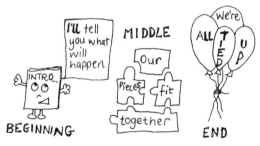

This will prevent your introduction becoming the essay, ensure the main body of your work flows, and allow you to draw a clear conclusion.

Making a diamond essay

Using a diamond structure will help you break the essay down into bite-sized pieces that will flow well when you put them all together. Here's how:

Imagine your whole essay as a that has:

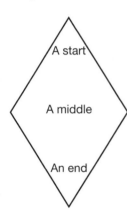

The **introduction** has its own structure and is **separate** from the **main body**.

The **main body** is the **development** of your **argument into clear sections** consisting of one or more paragraphs. Each of these paragraphs also has a start, middle and end.

The **conclusion** also has its own structure and purpose and is **separate** from the **main body**.

Thinking of your essay as a diamond will remind you that whatever *points you start, you have to finish off somehow*. This is the key to making your work flow.

A diamond essay: looking at the main body

Leave the introduction and conclusion for now and focus on the main body. This will be constructed of sections containing one or more paragraphs.

A **section** ◇ with one or more **paragraphs**

    will **link to** the **next section** ◇

        which **links to** the **next section** ◇

           ... and so on ... ◇

Until you get to the conclusion.

So all sections link together:

 link
link

A diamond essay: plan a perfect paragraph

Each **paragraph** will also follow our **diamond pattern**:

An opening sentence will be followed by supporting evidence and/or examples to back up your point. You may, of course, present an opposing argument, to show you are considering alternative viewpoints. You'll need to synthesise (put together) all this information to show that your argument is best. Let your reader know what you think in a mini conclusion, which may be your comment or a link to the next section.

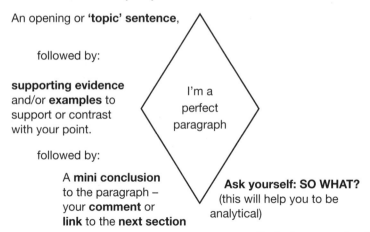

An opening or **'topic' sentence,**

followed by:

supporting evidence and/or **examples** to support or contrast with your point.

I'm a perfect paragraph

followed by:

A **mini conclusion** to the paragraph – your **comment** or **link** to the **next section**

Ask yourself: SO WHAT? (this will help you to be analytical)

Essay diamond

The stages of essay writing are:

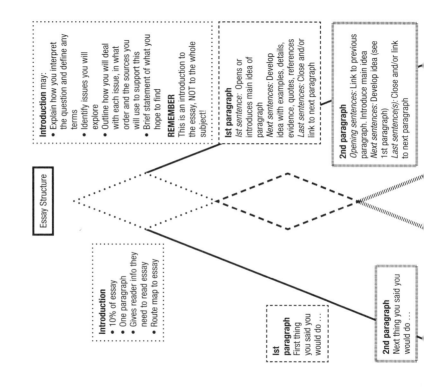

Essay Structure

Introduction may:
- Explain how you interpret the question and define any terms
- Identify issues you will explore
- Outline how you will deal with each issue, in what order and the sources you will use to support this
- Brief statement of what you hope to find

REMEMBER
This is an introduction to the essay, NOT to the whole subject!

1st paragraph
1st sentence: Opens or introduces main idea of paragraph
Next sentences: Develop idea with examples, details, evidence, quotes, references
Last sentences: Close and/or link to next paragraph

2nd paragraph
Opening sentences: Link to previous paragraph. Introduce main idea
Next sentences: Develop idea (see 1st paragraph)
Last sentence(s): Close and/or link to next paragraph

Introduction
- 10% of essay
- One paragraph
- Gives reader info they need to read essay
- Route map to essay

1st paragraph
First thing you said you would do …

2nd paragraph
Next thing you said you would do …

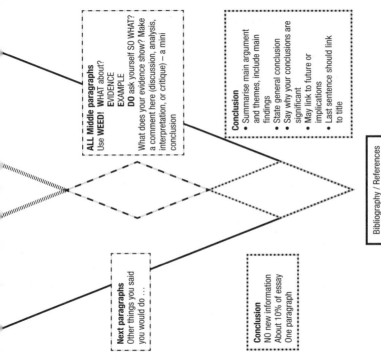

ALL Middle paragraphs
Use **WEED!** **WHAT** about?
EVIDENCE
EXAMPLE
DO ask yourself **SO WHAT?** Make
a comment here (discussion, analysis,
interpretation, or critique) – a mini
conclusion

Conclusion
- Summarise main argument
  and themes, include main
  findings
- State general conclusion
- Say why your conclusions are
  significant
- May link to future or
  implications
- Last sentence should link
  to title

Next paragraphs
Other things you said
you would do . . . .

Conclusion
NO new information
About 10% of essay
One paragraph

Bibliography / References

35

Use WEED to help you construct a paragraph

Every paragraph must make sense on its own. Your essay is really a string of paragraphs that should link together. Each paragraph should be making one point only.

WEED can help you remember what needs to be in **every paragraph**:

W is for **What**. Ask yourself: Have I made it clear what point I am making? This may also be called the 'topic sentence' as it signals the 'topic' this paragraph is about. You may have to **briefly explain** this.

E is for **Evidence**. Ask yourself: Have I provided supporting evidence for my point and/ or an alternative view? The evidence needs to be from your reading. It may be a theory, concept, model or idea. Check you have used reliable sources (see p. 87).

E is for **Example**. Ask yourself: Do I need to provide an example to illustrate the point I am making? If your essay title says 'with reference to' or 'give examples', then you should do this.

D is for **Do**. Ask yourself: What do I do with the information given? If you ask yourself '**so what?**', then you should be able to see why your point is important. Explain this to your reader. This is the analytical bit that will gain you those important extra marks.

Going deeper: the paragraph plan

Paragraphs are the building blocks of your essay. Use them properly and you are well on the way to constructing a good essay. **WEED** will help you remember the basics of a paragraph. The **paragraph plan** below goes into more detail about how to make a good paragraph.

The **first sentence** introduces the **point** that will be discussed in this paragraph. The **second sentence** explains or defines any **abstract, key or problematic terms**.

The **middle sentences** develop your point by providing:
supporting evidence for your point	**(essential)**
examples of this	(if needed)
an **alternative viewpoint**	(maybe)

Consider **what have you learnt?** Can you make **sense** of it? Try to put it all together (**synthesise ideas**).

The **final sentence(s) comments** on the evidence given, showing **what you have learnt**. Ask yourself **'so what?'** Show why or how this is important; this **puts your voice** in the essay.

Conclude by giving any **consequences or implications of your argument** and **link** these to the **next paragraph** as best you can. **Look back at the first sentence** of the paragraph to check you have **moved the argument on**.

Synthesising information

You may have noticed the word 'synthesising' in your assessment criteria – so what exactly does this mean?

Synthesising means actively thinking about the material you have presented and making some sense of it by drawing it all together so your reader can easily see where you have got to. If you have presented your evidence but left your reader to do all the hard work trying to work out what this all means, you will lose marks. Presenting too many ideas in a paragraph may confuse you, and your reader, so check you are only developing one point. The simple way to do this is to look at the first and last sentence of the paragraph to make sure they are connected. **Think carefully about the point you are trying to make, and consider if this is clear to your reader at the end of each paragraph.**

Example of a good paragraph

In Paul's paragraph example below, the highlighting corresponds to the four different parts of the paragraph.

What

Protocols detail a locally agreed framework for best care in a given circumstance, which should always be followed (NHS, 2006). Protocols also deliver a degree of legal protection for staff and patients (Grol et al., 2013) and provide consensus for the multidisciplinary team, which increases efficiency and saves time (NHS, 2006). NHS guidelines provide

Evidence

the best evidence-based advice in a given circumstance, which healthcare practitioners may apply (NICE, 2018). Failure to follow protocols can negatively affect the long-term outcome for patient recovery (CSP, 2016). Healthcare professionals and students may therefore use guidelines at their discretion but must follow protocols where they exist. The student's absence without notice could ultimately cause detriment to patient care.

Example

Other staff members may need to cover the student's responsibilities but this may be impossible at short notice with rising pressure on the NHS (NHS Employers, 2014). By neglecting a specific protocol, the student failed to provide the best quality of care. Failing to uphold responsibilities

Do

and follow instructions may also have created further stress for the clinical team, which ultimately causes both staff and service users to suffer.

What makes this a good paragraph?

W_{hat}
First sentence tells us the topic or point to be made in this paragraph.

E_{vidence}
Evidence from reliable sources to support the point made; the student also made a comment here to show his position.

E_{xample}
An example to illustrate. This is not always necessary, but if you are asked for an example or to use a case study, then you should try to integrate this.

D_o
Final sentence links to first 'topic' sentence. This sentence effectively comments on and concludes this paragraph. It needs to link to the next paragraph as best you can.

Understanding introductions and conclusions

Introductions and conclusions are the most important parts of your essay. Do not skimp on these. They provide the framework for your work and tell your reader what to expect, what you found out and the relevance of your findings.

Think of them as the bedposts of your essay.

Even if the middle section of your essay is not perfect (a bit lumpy perhaps), a good introduction and conclusion will provide the impression of a well-constructed essay.

What is the purpose of the introduction?

Remember, your introduction is an introduction to this essay only, not the whole topic.

Your essay introduction has three functions:

▶ to catch your reader's interest
▶ to provide your reader with any information they need to understand your work
▶ to tell your reader what you intend to cover and how you will do this. If you need to limit the focus of your essay, do it here.

Writing your introduction: what you need to include

An effective introduction will have **three aspects** to it. It needs to provide your reader with:

1 Any information needed to understand your work. This could be how you interpret the question, setting the scene with a brief background, and any definitions of terms in the title that need an explanation.

2 A route map to your essay. This sets out what you are going to do and how you are going to do it.

3 Say what you will argue. This is optional. You may not want to give the game away at the beginning, but it is a good idea for you and your reader to be clear about your viewpoint. This is sometimes called the 'thesis statement'.

So, producing a perfect introduction is as easy as:

    1 Information   **2** Route map   **(3?)** This essay will argue …

Introduction Part 1: information your reader needs to know

The introduction is the place to make sure your reader has all the tools they need to understand your work.

How you interpret the question

Just supposing you interpret the question slightly differently to your tutor? If you explain your understanding of the question to start with, at least they will know your starting point. You only really need to do this for a complex or ambiguously worded question. Unless you make a serious error here, this should not matter too much as long as you argue your case clearly.

Setting the scene with a brief background

This helps the reader to know what you consider the background to be and why this question needs to be addressed. Keep it brief, though. If you need to do a detailed background, this should become a section of the essay itself.

Definitions of terms in the title

Define any specialist or complicated words in the title. Your definitions will influence how you tackle the essay. If there is a debate about definitions in the literature, you may have to discuss this. If it is a lengthy discussion, make a brief reference to this in the introduction and discuss further in the first paragraph of the main body of the essay.

Introduction Part 2: what you are going to do and how this will be done

Tell your reader exactly what you are going to do and how you will do it. This gives your reader an idea of what to expect and shows you have a clear purpose. It also helps you to keep on track and work towards your conclusion.

Think of this as the *route map* to your essay:

What issues will you explore – *it is OK to* **define** *the* **limits** *of your essay, simply* **justify** *what you* **do** *cover*

in order to reach

your CONCLUSION

and exactly how you will do this.

Remember: everything in your essay should be working towards your conclusion. This does not mean you will not show the opposing view; only that when you do this, your viewpoint should be the stronger argument.

Introduction Part 3: say what you are going to argue

You do not *have* to do this. But if you do, your tutors will know **where you are going with your argument** and can focus on how you get there. They may appreciate not having to figure this out for themselves by rewarding you with a better mark. Some subjects, such as history, prefer this to be done.

Remember: your tutors want to see an argument and this will make it clear that they are getting one. It helps you clarify your own position and decide what your viewpoint really is.

And finally: a top tip about introductions

This may seem topsy-turvy but it is often better if you …

Write your introduction AFTER you have FINISHED the essay!

Why? Because as long as you know roughly what issues you are going to cover and how you will do this, you will only have to rewrite the introduction *to fit the essay you actually wrote*. This tip also stops the problem of your introduction becoming the essay itself because you fell into too much detail, too soon.

So, although the introduction is part of the essay, it is useful to think of it as a separate section, with its own structure and purpose.

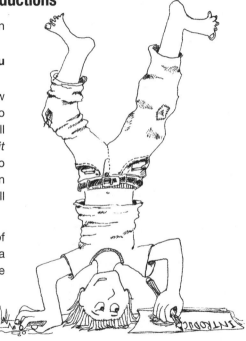

Has this student produced a good introduction?

Below is an example of a student's introduction to an essay with the title: *Can environmental problems be solved within the current structure of the global political economy?*

Take a look at the writing, compare it with what you know makes a good introduction and see if you agree with the comments. The highlighting corresponds to the different aspects of the introduction.

Aspect 1

The global economy can be caricatured as a wolf in sheep's clothing; a docile outer image concealing a ravenous predatory instinct. Our 'shepherding' of the global economy is increasingly called into question as the threats posed by untold environmental change become ever clearer. Debate surrounding the relationship between environmental degradation and global economic activity is divided between powerful advocates of the status quo, and those who believe that we must urgently intervene to curb environmentally damaging practices. This essay will argue that it is not possible to solve global environmental problems

Aspect 3

within the current structure of the global political economy because the principles that underpin the competitive free market unavoidably exploit it.

Analysis of student's introduction

Visual image, a good attention grabber.

Aspect 1   **Information reader needs.** Good background, makes it clear there are two viewpoints.

Aspect 2   **Route map of the essay.** There is NO outline of the issues to be covered or how this will be done.

Aspect 3   **Say what you will argue.** The writer's position is clear, but it would be good to know what principles are being referred to here.

Did the student write a good introduction?

The student did write a good introduction, but it could be improved slightly.

It is a good introduction because:
- It got the reader interested from the first sentence.
- It provided the information and background the reader needed to understand the context (**Part 1**, see p. 44).
- The writer has clearly stated what they will be arguing (**Part 3**, see p. 46).

It could be improved by:
- Although the writer's position (**Part 3**, see p. 46) is clear, we don't know exactly what issues will be explored and how this will be tackled. Giving a route map or guide of exactly what will be covered in the essay and saying how this is going to be tackled would have solved this (**Part 2**, see p. 45). For instance, the writer may have used a company case study to illustrate the essay, or may have set some limit on the scope of the essay by examining one particular environmental issue. The introduction is the place to make this clear.

Writing the conclusion: its purpose

What is the purpose of the conclusion?

Your conclusion has four functions:

1 To present your *main findings*, which **MUST** be in your essay. Coming to a conclusion that is just not there **is the most common error** students make!
2 To provide your reader with *your conclusion* from the evidence you have presented.
3 To explain any *implications* or *recommendations* arising from your conclusion.
4 To *answer the question*: do this in the last sentence to give your reader a sense of completion.

Writing your conclusion: what you need to include

The conclusion must tie everything up for your reader and give them a sense of satisfaction that the question has been answered. An **effective conclusion** needs to provide your reader with these **five parts**:

1 **A recap of what the essay explores** (one sentence if possible).

2 **A summary of your main findings**. Your tutor does not want to go back through your essay to sift for what you found out. So, do the work for them by presenting an overview of the main takeaway points.

3 **A clear conclusion**. Now you must present *your conclusion* from the evidence you provided. Your tutor may have a different opinion to you, so check your *evidence* really does *support your conclusion*.

4 **The implications of your conclusion**. Looking to the future here shows your tutor not only that can you argue your way to a conclusion but that you can also relate this in practice. Show how your conclusion(s) impacts, influences or is important in practice.

5 **An answer to the question!** Make the last sentence link directly to the title or question; this creates a sense of completion for your reader.

What NOT to do in the conclusion

There are two things to be aware of about conclusions:

    1 No new information   2 Your evidence must support your conclusion

An example of an unsupported statement in a conclusion: *'Our world is heavily over-populated ...'*. The student put this in the main text with no supporting evidence and repeated it the conclusion; this earned the rebuke 'prove it' from the tutor.

If you come to a **conclusion that is not supported by your evidence** or is simply not in your essay, **you are in big trouble**. It is OK if you ended up somewhere else, but you must show *how* you got there.

Do not put *any* new information in the conclusion. This is because you cannot provide the supporting evidence for it in the conclusion. You **may**, however, **point out any implications** of your conclusion or **make a recommendation** for future practice or suggest an action to make.

Tutors are not always concerned about the right answer, but they *are* really **interested in your ability to take a view and argue your way towards your conclusion.** They also want to see that you have used reliable evidence and examples (see p. 89), referenced these correctly (see p. 105) and used an appropriate academic style (see p. 114).

And finally: a top tip about conclusions

This may seem a bit strange but it is a good idea to:

Write a draft conclusion BEFORE you start the essay!

Why? Because it is much easier to argue your way through the essay if you have a rough idea of where you are going. You would not set out on a long journey without a destination (and hopefully a map – your plan in the case of an essay). Of course, you may not know what your conclusion is when you start, but as soon as you have an idea about this make a note of it. Doing this will help you focus throughout the essay and also enables you to spot when you are wandering off the point.

Remember: everything in the essay should **support your conclusion**. You **present alternative viewpoints** to show your argument is best and critique the evidence to **support your argument**.

 The conclusion should 'mirror' the introduction. Put these side by side when you write the conclusion. You should then clearly see where everything you said you would do in the introduction went.

Should mirror

Has this student produced a good conclusion?

Below is an example of Rosie's conclusion to an essay with the title: *To what extent did the Catholic Church perceive heretical movements as threats between c.1350–1517?*

Take a look at the writing below, compare it with what you know makes a good conclusion and see if you agree with the comments. The highlighting corresponds to the different aspects of the conclusion.

Aspect 3
Clear conclusion

Aspect 2
Sum up main points

Aspect 4
Future implications

In conclusion, the Lollard and the Hussite movements were perceived as threats to the Catholic Church as the works of the leaders became heretical yet they were accepted as successful movements. The Hussite movement lasted longer as it was able to gain the support of the Bohemian authorities. This set the precedent of a systematic church being able to function outside the Catholic Church ... The heretical movements were important as they laid the foundations for a systematic reform that had an impact on the religious authority as seen with the rise of the Lutheran Reformation.

Aspect 2
Sum up main points

Aspect 5
Answer the question

It was clear that the Catholic Church perceived these movements as a threat but only as they were not able to revert Bohemia to the Papal authority. This shows the controversies and religious discontent within society at the time of these religious movements. Overall, the Lollard and the Hussite movements were clear threats to the religious authority of the Catholic Church, which the authorities did recognise at the latter part of the 15th century.

Did the student write a good conclusion?

The student did write a good conclusion, but it could be improved slightly.

It is a good conclusion because:
- It answered the question (were clear threats …).
- It came to a conclusion (were perceived as threats).
- It gave a summary of the findings in the essay.
- It gave some of the implications (laid the foundations …; had an impact …).

It could be improved by:
- Recapping briefly what the essay covered.
- Checking that the conclusion 'mirrors' the introduction: that is, it matches what you said you would do in the introduction.

Notice that it did not matter that the student didn't put all the parts in the order on p. 52; just that they were all there. It is a good idea to say what the essay explored at the beginning of your conclusion.

Introductions and conclusions checklist

Does your introduction …	Yes	No
Use words and phrases from the title and/or the assignment brief?		
Indicate the main areas of your discussion?		
Show you know what issues apply?		
Make it clear what you did and didn't cover (useful if you need to limit the scope of the essay)? Give reasons for your decision.		
Make sure everything is linked to the question?		
Say what you will argue or state your position (optional)?		
Follow the introduction 1, 2, (3?) (see p. 43)?		
Does your conclusion …	Yes	No
Recap what you looked at (in one or two sentences)?		
Summarise your main findings?		
State a clear conclusion that follows from the evidence in the essay?		
Outline any implications of your conclusion? Look to the future here.		
Contain new ideas? Unless they are implications or ideas for future research, no new information in a conclusion, please.		
Mirror your introduction? Look at the introduction and conclusion side by side: do they fit together? Did you do what you said you would do?		
Answer the question directly – possibly in the last sentence?		

Adapted from Williams (1995)

What TYPE of essay are you doing?

Check your essay title for clues here. See if you can match up what you are being asked to do with the essay types below:

Argue   Discuss, judge, evaluate, advocate, analyse. Includes 'To what extent …' essays where you must finish by stating clearly the extent to which you think something is true or has happened.

Inform   Describe, review.

Compare/contrast   Identify two or more areas and show where they are similar and where they are different.

Reflect   Examine an incident/experience, and analyse how you reacted to inform your future practice and professional development.

Cause and effect   Examine why something happened (the cause) and the result (effect).

Planning an argument essay

In an argumentative essay you will be expected to take a viewpoint. You will have to identify points for and against your viewpoint and argue your way towards proving that yours is the more valid argument.

To start, note down:

My **argument will be** that …

Points *for* this	Evidence and examples
1	
2	
3	

Points *against* this	Evidence and examples
1	
2	
3	

Discussion	Strengths of my argument
	Weakness of my argument
	Weakness of other argument(s)
	Strengths of other argument(s)

Planning a 'to what extent' essay

This is essentially an argument essay, but in your conclusion you will have to make a judgement on how much or how far you agree or disagree with something. As with an argument essay, you are expected to take a viewpoint and identify points for and against this.

Start by working out just how far you agree or disagree with the proposition in your question by using a continuum line.

Example question: *To what extent can we explain the persuasive role of advertisements in terms of the elaboration likelihood model?*

Adapted from Williams (1995)

This is your conclusion, so work yourself there using the structure given for an argument essay. Make sure it *is* clear to what extent you agree/disagree with the statement in the question: to some extent, to a large extent, not at all, yes completely or anywhere in between.

Planning an informative essay

For this type of essay you will be expected to present facts or information. You may be asked to describe or review something. An informative essay should be written in direct language and should present material in an orderly way. You may need to evaluate which aspects are most significant and you will need to have data to support, clarify and give authority to your work. As always, you should only use reliable sources (see p. 89).

You will also need to decide how you will organise your material.

Ideas include:

- Divide into topics, themes or issues; deal with them in order of importance.
- Start with the broad or general picture, then become more specific or detailed.
- Be chronological: present information in the order it happened.
- Conclude by identifying the most significant aspects and look ahead to any implications these may have for the future.

Planning a compare and contrast essay

In a compare and contrast essay you will be expected to identify themes that are similar or different and explain the importance of these. Try using a Venn diagram (shown below) as a thinking and planning tool. Put differences in the outer circles and similarities in the middle where the circles overlap.

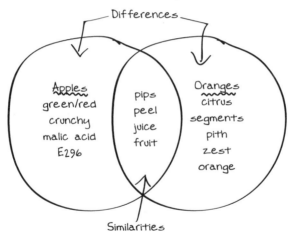

SCORE (2006)

Structure of a compare and contrast essay

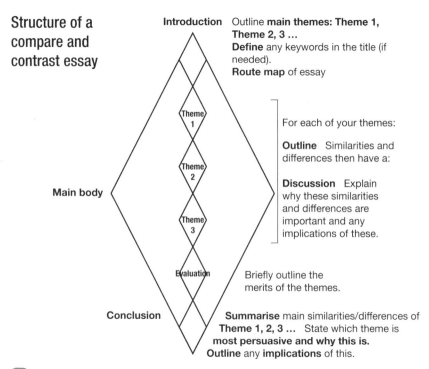

Introduction Outline **main themes: Theme 1, Theme 2, 3 …**
Define any keywords in the title (if needed).
Route map of essay

Theme 1

Theme 2

Theme 3

Evaluation

For each of your themes:

Outline Similarities and differences then have a:

Discussion Explain why these similarities and differences are important and any implications of these.

Main body

Briefly outline the merits of the themes.

Conclusion **Summarise** main similarities/differences of **Theme 1, 2, 3 …** State which theme is **most persuasive and why this is.** **Outline** any **implications** of this.

Planning a reflective essay

The reflective essay will expect you to examine an incident or experience you have had and to analyse how you reacted to inform your future practice. You will examine your strengths and identify areas where your performance needs development. You will use your reading to inform you and support your reflection. This type of essay is often set in fields such as healthcare, social work and education where you need to demonstrate competences and continuing professional development. Often, you will be asked to use a specific reflective model such as Gibbs (1988), Kolb's experiential learning (1984) or Honey and Mumford's (1986) learning cycle. Whatever model you use, it will have the following aspects and you can use this as a thinking and planning tool.

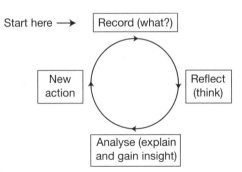

Start here ⟶ Record (what?)

Reflect (think)

Analyse (explain and gain insight)

New action

Copyright © 2014 RMIT University. Developed by the Study and Learning Centre, RMIT University

For more information, see *Reflective writing* in this series.

 Consider carefully the experience you will reflect on; it **must** allow you to be able to focus on some of the **course themes**. You still have to link the theory with the experience you are reflecting on. Avoid tackling too many themes.

Using a reflective model will help you analyse, reflect and develop an action plan for the future. In this type of essay the use of first person (I, my) is acceptable. You must relate your experience/practice to the literature available in the subject area. It may be useful to remember that in a reflective essay something must change by the end of it. You need to show how your research has informed how your future performance will change in response to what you have learnt.

The reflective essay is designed for you to use your experience and analyse this. You may have to challenge your beliefs, values, attitude and actions. You need to demonstrate why the experience/incident had a significant impact on your personal and professional learning and present an **action plan** to achieve this.

If you have to include an action plan, **SMART** objectives can be useful.

Objective	How do I show this in my work?
S = Specific objective	Use precise wording.
M = Measurable	Say how you will evaluate/or measure your success.
A = Achievable	Outline the resources and support you will require to make your action plan work.
R = Relevant/realistic	Say why/how the objective is important to your goal(s).
T = Timescale	Give an idea of how long all this will take.

Adapted from Bournemouth University (2006)

Structure of a reflective essay

Introduction

▸ **Outline** why **reflection is important** to your field.
▸ **Define** any **keywords** in the title (if needed).
▸ **Route map** of essay – identify the incident/experience, state any reflective model you will use to analyse this and say how your action plan will be presented.

Main body

▸ Outline the incident, be objective and **briefly explain** any reflective model you are using, one paragraph only.
▸ Next, you can *either*:
  ▸ use the steps in the reflective model *or*
  ▸ use the stages of the incident and fit the model in as you go.

Remember: in both cases **link your reading in**.

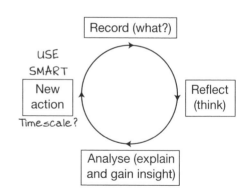

Conclusion

▸ **Summarise** the main points that arose from your essay and **identify areas you need to develop in future**.

▸ **Present an action plan** to show how you would tackle the situation next time; this shows what you have learnt. The action plan may have a timescale and use **SMART** objectives. Refer to, and follow, any guidance given.

Planning a cause and effect essay

In a cause and effect essay you will be expected to say why something happened (the cause) and what the result of this was (the effect). If there are a lot of possible causes and effects, you may have to limit yourself to a few main ones. This is fine as long as you make it clear in your introduction which ones you are leaving out (or, if shorter, the ones you are including). Check your essay title and any learning outcomes – you have to ensure you are not missing out an important cause/effect.

If you are finding it hard to decide which ones to include, go for the most recent or most direct causes and effects. Decide if you are aiming simply to inform or whether you need to persuade your reader, as this will affect the language you use. After providing evidence and examples of causes and the effect(s), it is a good idea to finish by showing what could be done differently – a call for action – but keep a professional tone with this.

- If there are **multiple causes,** you can deal with them one at a time: cause 1, then cause 2, then cause 3.
- For a **single cause** with multiple effects, use a new paragraph for each effect.
- For a **chain reaction,** follow the order of events, use a chronological (time) framework.

Structure of a cause and effect essay

Introduction

- **Identify the main causes and effects** you will cover using the words 'cause' and 'effect'.
- **Define** any **keywords** in the title (if needed).
- Provide a **route map** of the essay. It should be clear whether you are writing to **inform** or **persuade**.

Main body

This may be ordered in *one* of the following ways:

- **Chronological:** when the events occurred
- **Order of importance:** most/least or vice versa
- **Themes:** dividing the topic into parts or categories.

Try using a grid to sort your ideas out.

The cause: why something happened	The effect: the result of this	Conclusion: is this an important cause?	What next: a call for action?

Conclusion

Summarise the main causes and the effects of these. State **which cause** you think is most important and **why** (use evidence from the essay). Do you have a **call for action** to make? Keep your cool!

Planning a case study

In a case study it can be hard to balance explaining theory or models and linking these to your case study. If you are a business student and you are investigating the human resource practices of a particular company, then you must keep referring to the company. The idea is that you show you understand the theoretical concepts of your course by illustrating how they do (or don't) work in your chosen case study.

Structure of a case study

Introduction
» **Identify the case study and introduce the concepts/theories** you will cover. Provide a brief description of the case study (or if it is long you could put it in an appendix and say 'See Appendix 1'; check if this is OK with your tutor though).
» **Define** any **keywords** in the title (if needed).
» Provide a **route map** of the essay.

Main body

Introduce one aspect at a time. For **each paragraph**, use this general structure:

▸ **Outline** the theory/concept/model.
▸ **Analyse** how the case study fits/does not fit with these.
▸ **Comment** on what this means for the case study.

Conclusion

Summarise how well the case study matched with the theories/models discussed. Do you have **any recommendations** for the case study? You may be asked to present an **action plan** – if so, **SMART objectives** may be useful (see above).

See *Analyzing a case study* in this series for more on writing case studies.

Are exam essays different?

Yes, exam essays are different. You are working to a strict timescale and will only have access to what you can remember, unless it is an open book exam. Nevertheless, much of the process is the same as writing a coursework essay. Try the following procedure.

Before the exam

Check the exam format so you can divide your time up. Find out:

▶ How long will the exam be? Do you have any reading time?
▶ How many questions will you have to answer?
▶ Are there any limits? For example: Answer one question from Section A and four from Section B.
▶ Are marks allocated to questions? If so, use this to divide up your time.

Section A and B = 50% each.
Exam 2½ hours = 150 minutes
150 mins - 30 mins for reading, planning and proofreading = 120 mins
120/2 = 60 mins each for Section A and B
Section A = 60 mins for one essay question
Section B = 60/4 so 15 mins per question (12.5% each)

In the exam

You will write a much better, more coherent answer if you spend a few minutes at the start of the exam planning your time, analysing the question and doing a quick plan. This will prevent you from wasting time and possible marks by just writing down anything you can remember on the subject and expecting the poor marker to sift out any relevant information.

Step 1: Plan your time

Quickly check that the exam format has not changed from your expectation. Recalculate your timings if it has changed; double-check this.

Exam 2hrs = 120 mins - 20 mins (reading, planning
and proofreading) = 100 mins
100/2 = 50 mins each section
Section A = 50 mins for one essay question
Section B = 50/4 = 12 mins for each question (12.5% each)

Step 2: Analyse the question (also see pp. 22–3)

▸ Identify the process or instruction word (*discuss,* *outline,* *critically analyse*)

▸ What is the main subject or content?

▸ Are there any limits in the question?

▸ Any other aspects.

Discuss the factors that a team need to consider
when designing a health promotion programme.

Step 3: Do a two-minute plan

Really, this will help: spend two minutes getting down anything you think is relevant. Now go back to the question – is there anything you missed? Carefully check the instruction word; this tells you the detail to go into. Are there two parts to the question? Mind map, bullet point or just scribble, but do it! Reread the question once you have done this; make any adjustments necessary and then try to put your points in order. Just write a number beside each and cross out anything you won't have time to do. Now you have your plan.

<u>Intro</u> - 5 mins
- Why health prog important
- Identify factors

<u>Middle</u> - 40 mins
Factor 1.⎤
Factor 2.⎟ Outline each and how affects
Factor 3.⎦ prog design

<u>Conclusion</u> - 5 mins
- Main points and implications for prog design

Whatever else you do, **stick to your time and plan**. If you are running out of time, make a few bullet points about what you would have mentioned, leave space in case you get time to return to the question later, and move on to the next question.

Turning your plan into an essay

Very briefly, you will probably be doing the following.

Quick introduction

Be careful – don't let this become the essay:

▶ Brief background about why the subject is important.
▶ Brief outline of what you will discuss.
▶ Definitions.

Five/six paragraphs: one for each point from the plan you are making. Follow the **paragraph plan** (p. 37) or use **WEED** from the essay diamond (**W**hat, **E**vidence, **E**xample and **D**o, see p. 36) for an easy way to remember what to put in a paragraph.

Conclusion:

▶ Sum up the main points (probably one from each paragraph).
▶ State your overall conclusion; finish with any implications or action points of your conclusion – ideally you are looking to the future here.

Next question: plan and produce your answer using the same process.

Allow 10 minutes at the end of the exam **to proofread**.

After the exam

First, forget it for now. It is over: go off and celebrate or commiserate as appropriate!

When you get the result

Hopefully it will be good, or at least good enough, but you can learn a lot by reflecting honestly now on the experience while it is still fresh in your memory. Did any of the following happen?

▶ Ran out of time.
▶ Answered the question you wanted to see, not the one actually asked.
▶ Misread instructions.
▶ Did the wrong number of questions.
▶ Spent too long on one question, so didn't do justice to the others.

For my next exam I will …

Using the list on the previous page, note down **what actually happened**.
Spent too long on Section A question (1 hr 15 mins) so only did three questions from Section B & not the four I should have done.

Take a minute to think **what you are going to do** about this for next time.
I will work out time for each question and stick to it. Use bullet points & leave a space to return to if time. MOVE on to NEXT question on time.

Remember: everyone makes mistakes. What is important now is that you learn from your experience, so that you can improve for next time. This is how you can benefit from previous errors. If you don't reflect on what went well and what did not, you are likely to repeat the mistake. So be positive here and improve your grades.

Getting started is hard to do …

You will probably put this off for a while; after all, you have lots of time to do the essay. Then the moment of truth comes: the essay is due in soon and you have it all to do!

Look back to your **timeline** (p. 15). How much time do you really have? Do the preliminary groundwork (**collect all the information you need together**, p. 9), **dividing up your word count** (p. 19) and **analysing your question** (p. 22) as early as you can to break this cycle.

The next step is to get your **first thoughts** down and you can do this any way you like. The idea of this is just to put down anything you know about the subject, as quickly as you can. It gets you over the 'blank page' stage that can be paralysing. Try it out using the following steps:

1 Just get it down (anyhow – see opposite).
2 Add in any gaps in your knowledge or questions you have.
3 Cross out anything you think is not relevant.
4 Colour-code similar themes (just circle them for now).

First thoughts: ways to get them down on paper

BRAINSTORMING

MIND MAPPING

FREE WRITING

EXPLAINING TO A FRIEND

Still stuck?

Try answering these questions:
Who … Where … Why …
What … When …
Or talking it through with a friend, record your thoughts, tell the cat!

If you don't like using paper and pen, try using the computer. Mind-mapping programs such as MindView or Inspiration may help. Take a look at

mind mapping on the excellent website DnA at https://diversityandability. com/resources, where there are a variety of free mind-mapping programs to choose from.

Researching 83

What is the advantage of using mind-mapping software?

Programs such as MindView and Inspiration allow you to plan visually using a variety of colours, shapes and word art or graphics from a picture library or the internet to produce a mind map.

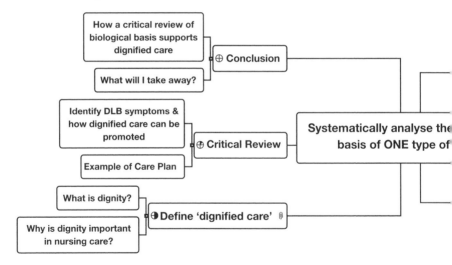

Nicky (Healthcare) used MindView to plan her essay. She broke it down into sections and added the questions and information she needed to find out so she didn't lose track. The little clocks in the boxes tell her how much she has done. She can link in other documents and websites as she develops her mind map plan.

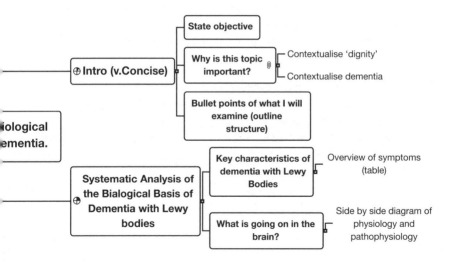

Converting mind map and outline to a document for editing

You can then convert your **mind map**, with the **outline of headings**, notes and web links you created, into a **Word document**. This Word document will contain your mind map (as a picture) with the outline *that you can then edit*. Just select the mind map picture and delete it before you hand the work in. Some programs allow you to convert your mind map to PowerPoint presentations, PDFs, flow charts and Gantt charts, and to add attachments such as Word documents, notes and hyperlinks.

 You get a 30-day free trial download of the latest version of Inspiration from www.inspiration.com, MindManager from www.mindjet.com and MindView from www.matchware.com. These programs are the most widely used in education. Do also look on your app store for mind-mapping apps – these are useful when you are on the go.

Information audit

OK, it is time to get down to work. By now you should have your:

▶ **word count** breakdown
▶ **analysis of the question, any learning outcomes, assessment criteria**
▶ **first thoughts**: colour-coded themes, questions and crossings out.

Gather these together; now do an information audit to identify what information you need to find out (research).

Use a grid (see below) to write down any themes you can identify from your first thoughts and fill in the information as fully as you can. This will produce a guideline of what you know (and what you don't). It may also highlight areas that will be hard to find evidence for, so you can consider whether or not to include these.

Theme	Keywords	Evidence for	Evidence against	Example

This will be useful for **planning the paragraphs** of your essay later on as it will provide all the information you need for the **paragraph plan** (see p. 37).

Gathering information

In professional courses, such as healthcare, business and education, there are usually two aspects to information gathering:

1 You will recognise that you are expected to produce *evidence of your reading and studying*. This research is the **theory** of your subject and includes the concepts, models and ideas of the key players in your field.

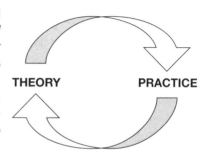

2 The **practical application** of this knowledge. Usually, you will be asked to examine a scenario and link the 'theory' you have learnt to your professional practice.

Other courses do this slightly differently as they require the application of knowledge (theory) to inform understanding (practice). For example, in history of art, the theory you learn will inform how you see or understand a painting in practice. All courses have these components.

This is what your tutor will want you to demonstrate in your essay.

Look back at your information audit and adjust it with this in mind.

How reliable is your evidence?

Where are you going to get the information you need? You will need to refer to **reliable sources** such as *textbooks*, *journal articles*, *published statistics*, *official publications* and *publications from professional bodies and organisations*. These sources will have been peer reviewed by professionals; that is, they have been read and checked by others working in the same research area and are regarded as reliable.

Sources such as *Wikipedia* and *some websites* are **regarded as unreliable**, as you cannot always check who wrote the information or whether it is accurate or not. It has not been peer reviewed so its reliability is in question. Use Wikipedia to find initial information, but you must move on to more reliable sources to use and reference these. Newspapers and radio programmes may alert you to issues you can follow up, or they may provide illustrations of a trend or viewpoint. They are not, however, reliable evidence of 'fact' or high-quality research. For this you need the genuine research itself.

There are times, though, when the use of sources that are considered unreliable is useful, for instance for a very current issue where limited research has been done. In this case, do acknowledge that you understand the source is not an academic source, and make sure you have not missed any reliable research.

Use AABBCC to check out the reliability of your sources – especially when evaluating web pages:

Accuracy   Authority   Bias   Breadth/depth   Currency   Compare

Adapted from Howe (2001)

Check your sources now: it's as simple as AABBCC

- **Accuracy**: Check the accuracy of the information you find. Can you find the same information elsewhere? Did the author reference it? Does it 'fit in' with what you already know? If it 'feels' wrong, it probably is.
- **Authority**: It is best if the author of your source is a well-known expert or organisation, then you can be sure they know what they are talking about. Check the website pages to establish who wrote it and if they wrote any other printed material you can find.
- **Bias**: Is the author trying to sell something – a product or a viewpoint? Check who wrote it. A drug company will not be negative about its product, will it? But a research organisation might be.
- **Breadth/depth**: Is the information detailed enough? Is evidence provided to back it up? It is good practice to fill in any missing gaps from other sources.
- **Currency**: Is the information up to date? If not, can you find more recent sources? Tutors like journal articles because they are up to date. Web pages are especially hard to find dates for – check the properties or 'page info' option, but beware: being up to date is no guarantee of accuracy.
- **Compare**: Compare your information with other sources; this will help you have confidence in it. It will also have the benefit of showing you a range of views – useful for your essay – and sources for your reference list.

Adapted from Howe (2001)

Sources checklist

Note: you need to be able to **tick** the **shaded boxes**.

	Yes	No
Accuracy Can you find the same information elsewhere? Did the author reference it? Does it 'fit' with what you already know?	Yes	No
Authority Is the author an expert or a respected organisation? View web pages/databases to find who wrote it; can you find anything else they wrote in a respected publication?	Yes	No
Bias Is the author trying to sell something – a product or a viewpoint? You need the answer to be 'No' here.	Yes	No
Breadth/depth Is the information detailed enough? Is evidence provided to back it up?	Yes	No
Currency Is the information up to date?	Yes	No
Compare Can you compare your information with other sources?	Yes	No

Adapted from Howe (2001)

WE THINK....

OLD SOURCES

Being critical, or, what do *you* think?

Your feedback may point out the need to be critical or it may suggest you used too much description in your work.

Use positive feedback

Nice point, well developed.

Good critique here.

 Most students focus on negative feedback, but try to use positive feedback too.

In academic writing your tutor wants to see you have read the literature, understood it and *also* that you have come to your own viewpoint. Yes, really! This is why just describing gets lower marks. Tutors want to hear what you have to say; however, this MUST be based on the reading you have done.

Notice in your work where your tutor made a positive comment and analyse what you did to please them. Nearly always, this is for going beyond the original idea and making it clear **what you think**.

The critical thinking model

The 'model to generate critical thinking' by John Hilsdon from Plymouth University shows how you need to move on from description to analysis so that you can then make an evaluation for yourself (Learning Development, 2006).

 There is a very useful two-page flyer of this, freely available online. Print out the model on the first page, and read the second page for some useful starter questions for analysing and evaluating. To access the critical thinking model, go to the Plymouth University website at www.plymouth.ac.uk/learn and scroll down for the Study Guides: www.plymouth.ac.uk/uploads/production/document/path/1/1713/Model_To_Generate_Critical_Thinking.pdf.

The flyer is shown opposite.

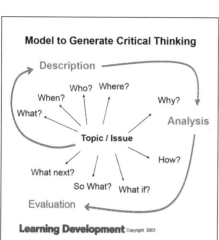

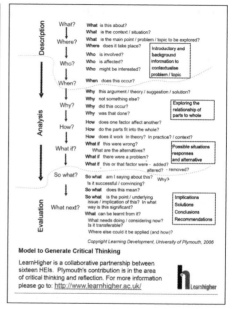

Plymouth University, Learning
Development (2006)

Analysing the critical thinking model

Look now at the critical thinking model. Notice it is divided into: Description, Analysis, Evaluation.

Also notice the words under each heading – these will indicate to you which stage you are at:

- **Description**: you are saying what, when, who or where. Simply providing information.
- **Analysis**: here you are using why and how words. How does it work? Why is it like this?
- **Evaluation**: now you are moving on from your analysis to suggest what this means (So what?), what may happen as a result of your findings and thoughts (What next?) and maybe suggest what could happen in a different situation or if something changed (What if?).

Now look at the second page of the model. You do NOT have to address all the questions, but they are useful starter questions for each of the stages. It is worth spending a bit of time really trying to see how the questions can lead you through the three stages of description, analysis and evaluation. When you are confident you understand this, move on to try using the model.

Using the critical thinking model

Description

Look around and describe the room you are sitting in … You have probably described the colour of the walls and flooring, and any windows and furniture in the room. This may not have told me much about the function of the room or whether it is fit for its purpose. For this you need to do more analysis.

Analysis

You need to ask more questions: *How* does it work? *How* many people use it? *Why* is it laid out as it is? *What* would happen if something changed and even more people needed to use it? Having asked these critical questions, you can now do an evaluation about the space and its suitability for its purpose. This is critical thinking.

Evaluation

This is where you show what your position is now, and this **MUST be drawn from your analysis of your reading**. You will have moved on from simply describing what you read. This has involved critical thinking to help you make more sense of the situation. Now you can judge the relative merits (or not) of the issue, which will lead you to *implications and conclusions*. For example, you may now see that although the room you are sitting is suitable as a student study room, it would be hopeless as a kitchen.

You are expected to do the same in your academic writing: not simply telling your reader what some researcher said (describing) but also analysing what was good, bad or odd about it so that you can evaluate how strong the evidence really is. You can then say something about it for yourself so that your reader knows you have done some real critical thinking, not just repeated information from your reading.

Try it yourself

Now try to think of an example of this from your own studies. Look at the last paragraph you wrote. If the purpose of it was simply to provide information, pick another paragraph where you needed to provide some analysis. Highlight descriptive text in a colour. Use the words above to identify this. Use another colour to show where there was some analysis using how and why type questions. Pick another colour to show what conclusion (evaluation) you came to.

If the descriptive colour is most of the paragraph, you may not have moved on to analysis. Look back at the analysis questions on the critical thinking model flyer to see if any help. At the very least, doing this exercise will draw attention to how effective you are at analysis. If this is still a problem, do look at *Getting critical* in this series to ensure you develop your critical skills and improve your grades.

Where do I show I am being critical?

Usually this will be after you have presented the main research ideas you have read about (you should reference these, of course).

The shaded areas in Hilary's essay (Nursing) show her critique:

Heyn et al.'s (2013) research showed patients did not always show clues, or they were ambiguous and were often missed in the consultation; instead, they were better at expressing their worries and fears. The source of hints can come from either the HCP who invites further disclosure or the patient, and the expression of ED can depend very much on the response of the HCP. Heyn et al.'s (2013) evidence shows that clues will occur within 5–10 minutes of the consultation and are more often expressed to nurses than doctors. Perhaps this is because patients felt more comfortable showing their ED, had an empathetic response or perhaps nurses could read and explore patients' clues, had education in holistic care and had better communicating skills. Nurses may, however, document ED but not address them possibly due to a lack of confidence and training (Heyn et al. 2012). Doctors failed to detect clues – was this due to time constraints, education or because they work with the biomedical model of assessing patient complaints and concerns, i.e. they work professionally differently? This research failed to establish how long patients and HCP had known each other, what their relationship was like, and all the data was collected by audio tape, not videotaped, possibly missing vital clues.

Language to show you are being critical

 Use the excellent Academic Phrasebank from Manchester University for a selection of useful starter phrases you can use in your work to introduce questions and limitations, make suggestions, and identify a study's weaknesses. See www.phrasebank.manchester.ac.uk/being-critical.

Showing your voice in your work, or, what do *I* think?

Your tutors want to see not only that you have read the relevant research and understood it, but also that you have formed an opinion about it. That is done by showing some critical thinking.

Your opinion must, of course, come from the *research evidence* and not just be random thoughts of yours. To be direct about it: your reader is not interested in your opinion *except in relation to the research evidence*. They *are* very interested in what you think about that.

This is why academics are so particular about referencing. They need to see where YOUR OWN THINKING is. If you reference properly, they can clearly see where you got your evidence from.

Anything not referenced is taken as your personal opinion, or possibly as having been reproduced from somewhere without you referencing it. This is why failing to reference properly (and clearly) indicates possible plagiarism.

Don't be scared about this. Learn to reference properly and show exactly what you think. You will be rewarded with higher marks for both these academic skills.

See also *Referencing and understanding plagiarism* in this series.

Check to see if you have taken a position and shown *your voice*

If you are still referencing at the end of a paragraph, it is quite likely that you have not moved on from describing someone else's idea. To show what you think, you will need to use such phrases as:

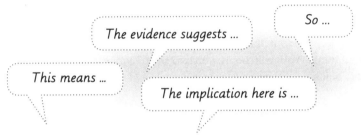

Because you are not referencing anymore, your reader knows it is *you* doing the speaking – literally showing your voice in the essay and making your position clear. You will be well rewarded for this.

The shaded sentence in the following essay by Michelle (Anthropology) shows what she thought:

Munro (2000) further explains how the local Scottish media portrays fishermen as either 'anti-social rule breakers, covertly landing illegal fish' or 'heroic, pre-industrial, hunter gatherers' (Munro, 2000, p. 8). Both of these descriptions unfairly portray the anachronistic attitudes that fishermen have been facing for years. MacLaughlin (2010) further elaborates on the marginalisation of fishermen during post-famine Ireland. Agrarian nationalism viewed Irish fishermen as the 'people of the rocks' and absent from the reform for national independence. Fishermen were pushed back into the corners, as the ruling class amassed more and more land under the notion that sedentary societies should have first claim to global resources (Laughlin, 2010, p. 335). Explanations for such ethnicism could be that gutting and flaying fish is 'dirty' and therefore is seen as an impure line of work. The precarious nature of fishing is superfluous and nomadic in that it is seen not to fit into industrial society.

Notice you do not say 'I think ...'. You should always use the third person for this – use phrases such as those shown in the speech bubbles on the previous page.

See *Writing for university* in this series. Section 5 shows what critical writing is and, more importantly, what it is not. Section 13 demonstrates how to show your own voice. Section 14 suggests language to use to show you are being critical.

Getting critical, in this series, shows the 'critical steps' and also illustrates what 'A'-grade critical writing looks like.

Academic Phrasebank is very helpful for starter phrases to help you support, contradict, advise caution about research, suggest implications or simply comment on any findings: www.phrase-bank.manchester.ac.uk/discussing-findings.

References, bibliographies and appendices

Referencing: why am I being asked to reference?

Referencing **shows your tutor** you:

- have research skills and can find information
- have read around the subject
- can provide evidence for the point you are making from your research
- can follow the referencing method for your subject.

Any university assignment requires you to read around your subject. Some fields such as healthcare focus on evidence-based practice (EBP).

EBP relies on you being able to:

1 Find reliable sources.
2 Critically evaluate what the research says.

AND

3 Assess the quality of the evidence.
4 Apply any findings you have made to your practice or practice area.

Assessment criteria ask you to demonstrate you have consulted a **range of academic literature**, refer to this in your own work correctly and provide a list of references.

When should I reference?

References are where you display to your reader what you have read and acknowledge the research other people have done.

If you use someone else's idea, *even if you put it in your own words*, you need to reference it. You do not need to reference general knowledge or information or knowledge generally known in your field. Specific information, such as statistics, must always be referenced.

Whose idea is it? Did you wake up this morning knowing this?

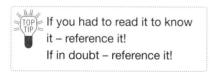

If you had to read it to know it – reference it!
If in doubt – reference it!

Can your reader track down your sources?

Your reader *must* be able to find your sources from the information you have given in your references. If there is any missing information, this may not happen.

Imagine your reader is on a treasure hunt – they need clues:

Clue 1 is a **short reference in the text** of your work near to where you have included the information from the source. This may be a name and date as in the Harvard system, or a number (which may have a footnote below) as in the British numeric system. The exact format depends on the referencing system you are using.

Clue 2 is a **full reference at the end** of your work, giving precise information.

Can your reader find your sources?

How to reference

There are **two aspects** to referencing; you **must do both** of these:

1 Put a **citation** in the **text** of your work – this is the **in-text reference**.
2 Provide a **full reference** somewhere – at the end of your essay for Harvard and numeric; other referencing systems vary, so double-check this.

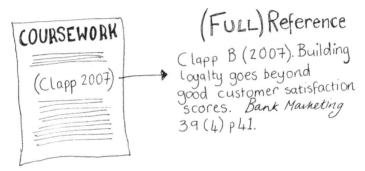

COURSEWORK

(Clapp 2007)

(FULL) Reference

Clapp B (2007). Building loyalty goes beyond good customer satisfaction scores. *Bank Marketing* 39 (4) p41.

> **TOP TIP** Whatever your university/course referencing system is, find it and familiarise yourself with it. Ask academic staff, study advice services or subject librarians for help if you need it. It will be worth the effort!

See *Referencing and understanding plagiarism* in this series.

What is the difference between references and bibliography?

1 **References**: Your list of references must contain *all* the **in-text references** (or **citations**) you have used **in the text of your work**.
2 **Bibliography**: This may include books, articles and various sources you have read but not referred to in your work. It has to be clear, however, which sources you used and which you did not. In this case you should **divide** the Bibliography into *References* (cited in your text) and *Other sources consulted* (which you read but did NOT actually use in YOUR work).

And finally: a note on plagiarism

All universities are concerned about plagiarism: this is where you copy information or use an idea without acknowledging where it came from.

Always keep a careful record in your notes of where you found information and include the page number in your draft versions. You only need to use the page number in your final draft if you quote directly, but it will help you if you need to recheck anything. Remember, it is far better to put the idea into your own words by paraphrasing as this clearly demonstrates your understanding and learning.

For more on referencing, see *Referencing and understanding plagiarism* in this series.

Referencing tips

- References need to be **COMPLETE**, **CORRECT** and **CONSISTENT**: *remember these 3 Cs for top marks.*
- Learn your referencing system and follow any guidance given.
- Be consistent: make a best guess of how to do it and then stick to this throughout your work.
- Beware of cramming too many references into a paragraph. It is easy just to say what other people said and did, but your reader needs to know *what you think, so show this*, before rushing off to find more sources.

For more on **being critical**, see *Getting critical* in this series.

For more on **referencing**, see *Referencing and understanding plagiarism* in this series.

Make referencing easier with online tools

Online tools to show you how to reference anything:

Cite them right: This is an excellent resource, use it! www.citethemrightonline.com.

Also useful are *referencing apps*, *reference generators* and *referencing management/ software* such as EndNote or Zotero. Search the internet or your app store for the terms in *italics* above and take your pick.

Appendices

Information essential to understanding your point should be in the main body of the essay. Only put something in an appendix that your reader may find useful; this should be specifically referred to in your text.

Appendices may include:
- supporting evidence
- field notes
- raw or processed data (summary should be in your main body text)
- questionnaires (results go in the main body of your text)
- detailed descriptions – research methods, for example
- technical figures, tables or descriptions
- maps.

Adapted from University of New England (2004)

Appendices should be arranged in the order they are referred to in the text. You can use numbers or letters. In your text simply put: '… (see Appendix 1) …'. Put each appendix on a new page and remember to add them to a contents list if you have one. Page numbers continue on from the main work. Provide a contents list at the start of your appendices if you have a lot of them. The appendix goes after the references.

Note: Appendices are not included in your word count, but this does not mean you should use them as a way to extend your word limit.

Only include things you have referred to in your work.

Academic style

You will be asked to use academic style, so what does this mean?

Be formal

- Don't write as you speak, **avoid colloquial (slang) and common phrases,** such as 'it went pear-shaped'. Instead, say 'it started to go wrong' or 'it developed problems'.
- Use the **full version of words**: 'have not' rather than 'haven't'.
- Always **explain abbreviations** the first time you use them: 'the National Institute for Clinical Health and Excellence (NICE) recommends …'.
- **Avoid sexist language:** chairperson not chairman.

Be remote

▶ **Avoid overusing** *I,* *we* **or** *you* **for personal opinions**: 'I think that …', 'We believe that …', 'You feel that …'.

This is not useful in an academic essay where you need to back up what you are arguing with evidence from the literature. Use the third person when analysing or commenting on the evidence to say how your view differs: 'The evidence suggests…', 'So … ', 'It is apparent that …'.

The exception to this is in reflective writing where it is acceptable to use 'I' or 'my'. When referring to the literature, though, it is still best to use the third person (it, the, the research). Check your guidelines.

▶ **Don't ask your reader questions**; they want answers. This writing style is better suited to journalism.

Be concise

▸ Long-winded explanations usually end up being descriptive. Focus just on the point you are trying to make. Short sentences are OK. Avoid long sentences: if your reader has to reread your work it will just irritate them. Most academic sentences are about 15–20 words long.

▸ **Give definitions** for technical or unusual terms unless your reader is expected to know them. Consider who your audience is.

▸ **Don't generalise –** for example, 'many people'. The following sentence appeared in a student essay: *Economy has played a big part in human existence.* This earned the tutor comment, 'This is excellent nonsense!'

▸ **Avoid vague terms** such as *nice*, *get* or *thing*.

Be cautious

▸ Say something **may** or **could** happen, *not* that it **will** (unless you can prove it, of course): 'This suggests …' or 'This indicates …'. Researchers are usually tentative when reporting their findings because research rarely proves something absolutely. So it is better to say that the research *shows*, *suggests* or *indicates* rather than it has *proved* something.

Using 'signal' words

Signal words indicate what you are doing and 'signpost' your reader through the different sections of your essay giving them a constant stream of clues to follow. If you leave these clues out, your reader may struggle to follow your argument. They may get confused and won't reward you with the marks your work really deserves.

Use words that signal clearly what you are doing.

Signal words explained

Signal word(s)	Purpose	Alternative words
First, Second, Third …	Show order of points made	in addition, next, then, to start/begin with, initially, additionally, lastly, moreover, subsequently, finally, previously
And	Adding extra points	also, and, in addition, then, again, furthermore, with regard to
For example	Introducing examples	for instance, in other words, including, the following, these include, that is, this demonstrates, such as, to illustrate this, namely
Another view	Show other views/opinions	in contrast, although, on the other hand, yet, alternatively, but, on the contrary, despite, conversely, whereas, even so, otherwise, however
As a result	Show the results or effect of something	therefore, as a result, so, thus, due to, consequently, because of this, it can be seen, the evidence shows, hence, this suggests, the implication is, one result is, as, inevitably

More signal words explained

Signal word(s)	Purpose	Alternative words
Emphasise	To stress a point	obviously, definitely, undeniably, inevitably, generally, admittedly, especially, clearly, importantly, in fact, indeed, in particular
Exceptions	To show exceptions	however, in spite of, yet, nevertheless
Equally	To show similarity	similarly, likewise, as well as, correspondingly, in the same way, also, just as
To compare	To compare with something else	just like, same as, similar to, not only … but also, compared to/with
Another cause	To show cause(s)	due to, because, another …, since, first, second
To conclude	To sum up points so far	in conclusion, to conclude, to sum up, to summarise, so, overall, consequently, as discussed, as has been shown

 Take care with *however*. It can be useful to signal a change of direction in your argument, but it is overused by students.

Making it flow: use signposts

Many students fill their essays with facts and references but fail to explain the relevance of these. If you do this, you are making your tutor do the job of trying to work out where you are going with your argument. Make your essay easy to read by using a few simple tricks to lead your tutor gently to your conclusion and you will be rewarded with those vital extra marks. As a bonus you may even need to do less research overall.

Simple tricks to make your essay flow

1 Use signposting throughout the essay.
2 Use paragraphs (see paragraph plan, p. 37 and essay diamond, p. 33).
3 Use signal words to 'signpost' your essay (see p. 118).
4 Outline your essay structure clearly in the introduction (see p. 45).
5 Make sure your conclusion 'mirrors' your introduction (see p. 54).
6 Refer to the title in the last sentence of the essay.

Problem solving

Too long: over word or page count

Make up your mind to work to your word count next time (see p. 19). Time was wasted on researching and writing and now more time is needed to cut your work back – so twice the work. But for now look out for and mark where:

- Information is **repeated**. Choose the best example and cut the rest out. This is hard to do as by now you love it, but just do it!
- More than one example is given – will one do? (Yes, usually!)
- **Part** of your essay **does not seem to fit in**. If it does not argue towards your conclusion, it may be irrelevant (unless it is a counter-argument you are dismissing). Consider cutting it out.
- You have gone **off track** or into too much detail. Are you **waffling** and not developing your point? Check the paragraph plan (see p. 37).
- You have **quoted**. Use paraphrasing and summarising – this uses fewer words and because they are your own words it **shows your understanding**. If you have quoted, have you also commented on what you think is important or special about the quote? A quote can't stand by itself.

Too short: under word or page count

- **Analyse your question** (p. 22) and recheck any information you have been given, the assessment criteria and the learning outcomes. If covering diversity or ethical issues is in these, for instance, they should appear in your work.
- Check that **every paragraph** follows the **paragraph plan** (p. 37).
- Ensure you have a strong **introduction** and **conclusion**. These are vital for your reader to understand your work (p. 41).

Always proofread your work

Read the following tutor's comment on a student essay. After you finish laughing, remember this is from a real student essay.

Tutor comment: 'note the difference between phatic and phallic … might lead to embarrassment!'

You may not have made an embarrassing error in your essay, but you will have made errors that you found hard to spot.

Try:

- Reading your work out loud. Use text-to-voice software. This is especially useful for dyslexic students.
- Asking someone with good English to read it. They do not have to be a subject specialist; if you have written it well, they will be able to follow it. Ask them to point out anything they do not understand; proofreading is not just about spelling, grammar and punctuation. You may have missed out relevant information.

 TOP TIP Leave your work for a few days and then read it through. This allows your memory of it to die back so you read what you actually wrote, not what you thought you wrote. A good reason to finish early!

And finally: check and recheck your references.

It is easy just to look at your final mark and ignore the comments on your work. Your tutors should give you valuable feedback. They spend time and effort on this and it is the key to improving your work. If you compare the comments you have received for different assignments, it is almost certain you will be able to see a pattern of your strengths and any concerns.

If you don't understand the feedback, do ask your tutor to explain it or visit any source of study advice available to you. This could be academic advisers, subject librarians or specialist support tutors if you have a specific learning difficulty.

Look at the following feedback comments on students' work. What are the most common problems?

Tutors' comments:
'So what does this tell us about the question?'
'You need to expand and justify your position.'
'Over two pages of description before we get to the question …'
'Lacks explanation and lapses into description.'

'Line of argument could have been tighter and more focused – set out your argument at the beginning and keep reminding us where you have got to.'

'Some sources quite old now.'

'What do *you* think? In end not sure what you think …'

'Need to criticise the models …'

'Some referencing issues …'

Using feedback to make an action plan

Try to look back at (or remember) some of your own feedback now. The same comments are likely to keep happening unless you try to change how you do things.

Which comments or problems above most closely match your own? Write them down now in an **action plan** like the one below.

| I need to improve … | the flow of my essay | I can do this by … | using signal words (see p. 117) |
| | conclusions | | using the conclusions checklist (see p. 58) |

Determine to 'action' your action plan for your next essay and see your grades improve. Use the following table of common problems and possible solutions for guidance.

The most common errors

Problem	Solution	See
Not answering the question	Analyse the question and make sure you keep referring back to it during the essay. Take special note of instruction or process words in the title.	**p. 22** **p. 24**
No structure/lack of organisation	Show you understand what is expected in the introduction and revise the paragraph plan to organise the main body. Review the essay diamond to check you understand essay structure. Check the conclusion has moved on from the introduction so you show what you found out. Check the drafting and redrafting section to improve the flow of your essay by using signposting and signal words.	**pp. 47–58** **p. 33** **p. 54** **p. 117**
Academic style	Familiarise yourself with academic style and use it. These are easy marks to get.	**p. 114**
Lack of evidence and critical skills	Avoid description. You must select **appropriate** evidence for your points with a model, theory or concept. Use a range of reliable sources. Provide examples if needed. Show the relevance of your evidence and example(s); this avoids 'collecting references' which won't always result in better marks.	**p. 91** **p. 88** **p. 89**

Problem	Solution	See
Referencing inaccurate	Know the system you should use and really learn it – these are easy marks to get. Always acknowledge your sources.	**pp. 105–11**
Referencing: overquoting	Review why it is best not to do this and learn to paraphrase effectively.	**p. 109**
Referencing: reliability of sources	Use AABBCC to check this.	**p. 90**
Lack of student voice	Make your position clear in the introduction. Make a comment about what you think of the evidence or any implications at the end of paragraphs. Your position must be also be clear in your conclusion.	**p. 46** **p. 92** **p. 102** **p. 52**

Essay-writing checklist

To finish off, let's return to Norton's (1990) essay-writing criteria (see p. 5), which show exactly what tutors want to see in student essays. This has been changed slightly so that you can use it as an essay-writing checklist.

Check you have …

Criteria	Tutors' ranking	Have you done this? yes/no	See
Answered the question	1		**p. 22**
Shown understanding	2		**p. 6**
Given an argument	3		**p. 60**
Provided relevant information	4		
Provided a structure with clear organisation of ideas	5		**p. 30** **p. 59**
Provided evaluation(s) or your own view	=6		**p. 94**
Followed academic style and presented your work as asked	=6		**p. 114**
Demonstrated wide reading	8		**p. 89**
Checked your English and spelling is correct (proofread your work)	9		**p. 123**
Shown content/knowledge	not ranked		

Adapted from Norton (1990)

References

Bournemouth University (2006) *Reflective writing*. Available at: www.bournemouth. ac.uk/study_support/reflective_writing.html (accessed 30/06/2008).

Elander J, Harrington K, Norton L, Robinson H and Reddy P (2006) Complex skills and academic writing: a review of evidence about the types of learning required to meet core assessment criteria. *Assessment and Evaluation in Higher Education*, 31(1): 71–90.

Gibbs G (1988) *Learning by doing: a guide to teaching and learning methods*. Oxford Further Education Unit, Oxford Polytechnic.

Howe W (2001) Evaluating quality. Available at: www.walthowe.com/navnet/quality. html (accessed 4/04/2019).

Learning Development (2006) *Model to develop critical thinking.* Flyer, Plymouth University. Available at: www.plymouth.ac.uk/uploads/production/document/ path/1/1713/Model_To_Generate_Critical_Thinking.pdf (accessed 18/04/19).

Mathnews (2000) *Amusing statistics*, 84(5). Available at: www.mathnews.uwaterloo. ca/Issues/mn8405/stats.php (accessed 29/12/2013).

Morley J (2013) *Academic phrasebank*. The University of Manchester, University Language Centre. Available at: www.phrasebank.manchester.ac.uk (accessed 4/04/2019).

Norton LS (1990) Essay writing: what really counts? *Higher Education*, 20(4): 411–42.

Price G and Maier P (2007) *Effective study skills*. Harlow: Pearson Education.

RMIT (2006) *The reflective cycle*. Available at: www.dlsweb.rmit.edu.au/lsu/content/2_AssessmentTasks/assess_tuts/reflective%20journal_LL/cycle.html (accessed 4/04/2019).

SCORE (2006) *Graphic organisers*. Available at: www.sdcoe.k12.ca.us/score/actbank/sorganiz.htm (accessed 3/07/2008).

University of New England (n.d.) *Appendices*. Available at: https://une.edu.au/__data/assets/pdf_file/0019/12772/WE_Appendices.pdf (accessed 16/04/19).

University of Southampton (2004) *Planning and writing your essay: an overview*. Available at: www.soton.ac.uk/studentsupport/ldc/docs/Essays%20text%202004.doc (accessed 4/04/2019).

Williams K (1995) *Writing essays*. Oxford: Oxford Centre for Staff Development.

Useful sources

Academic Phrasebank (2005) The University of Manchester, University Language Centre. Created by Dr John Morley. Available at: www.phrasebank.manchester.ac.uk (accessed 4/04/2019).

Cottrell S (2019) *The study skills handbook* (5th edn). London: Red Globe Press.

Godfrey J (2016) *Writing for university (2nd edn).* London: Red Globe Press.

Learning Development (2006) *Model to develop critical thinking.* Flyer, Plymouth University. Available at: www.plymouth.ac.uk/uploads/production/document/path/1/1713/Model_To_Generate_Critical_Thinking.pdf (accessed 18/04/19).

Pears R and Shields G (2019) *Cite them right: the essential referencing guide* (11th edn). London: Red Globe Press.

Williams K (2014) *Getting critical* (2nd edn). London: Red Globe Press.

Williams K and Davis M (2017) *Referencing and understanding plagiarism* (2nd edn). London: Red Globe Press.

Index